W9-BXZ-073

The ESSENTIALS® of
REGISTERED TRADEMARK

ACCOUNTING I

Duane R. Milano, Ph.D.
Professor of Accounting
East Texas State University, Commerce, Texas

Charles S. Robnett, M.B.A.
East Texas State University, Commerce, Texas

This book covers the usual course outline of Accounting I. For additional topics, see *"THE ESSENTIALS OF ACCOUNTING II."*

Research & Education Association
61 Ethel Road West
Piscataway, New Jersey 08854

THE ESSENTIALS®
OF ACCOUNTING I

Printed in the United States of America

Library of Congress Catalog Card Number 98-66387

International Standard Book Number 0-87891-667-9

ESSENTIALS is a registered trademark of
Research & Education Association, Piscataway, New Jersey 08854

WHAT "THE ESSENTIALS" WILL DO FOR YOU

This book is a review and study guide. It is comprehensive and it is concise.

It helps in preparing for exams, in doing homework, and remains a handy reference source at all times.

It condenses the vast amount of detail characteristic of the subject matter and summarizes the essentials of the field.

It will thus save hours of study and preparation time.

The book provides quick access to the important facts, principles, theorems, concepts, and equations in the field.

Materials needed for exams can be reviewed in summary form – eliminating the need to read and re-read many pages of textbook and class notes. The summaries will even tend to bring detail to mind that had been previously read or noted.

This "ESSENTIALS" book has been prepared by an expert in the field, and has been carefully reviewed to assure accuracy and maximum usefulness.

Dr. Max Fogiel
Program Director

CONTENTS

CHAPTER 1

INTRODUCTION

1.1 DEFINITION OF ACCOUNTING

Accounting can be described as an information system that provides essential information about the financial activities of a business entity to various individuals or groups for their use in making informed decisions.

Accounting is primarily concerned with the design of the recordkeeping system, the preparation of summarized reports based on the recorded data, and the interpretation of those reports.

1.2 USERS OF ACCOUNTING INFORMATION

Users of accounting information can be quite varied, depending on the type of decision under consideration. Accounting information might be used for decisions involving investments, to impose income taxes, or for regulatory or managerial decisions. The process of using accounting to provide information to users is illustrated in Chart 1.2.1.

As shown in this diagram, the first step is to identify user needs. A properly designed accounting system can then generate summarized reports (using recorded transaction data) to meet those needs for accounting information. Users can then use those reports to make informed business decisions.

CHART 1.2.1

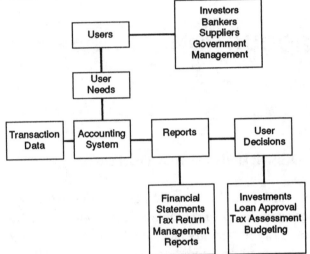

1.3 GENERALLY ACCEPTED ACCOUNTING PRINCIPLES

This broad range of potential users has brought about the evolution of Generally Accepted Accounting Principles (GAAP) used in preparation of financial statements. Many of these principles have been formally established by standard-setting bodies such as the Financial Accounting Standards Board (FASB). Others have simply gained acceptance through widespread use. Adherence to GAAP provides a measure of consistency in preparation of financial statements.

1.4 THE ACCOUNTING EQUATION

Assets are tangible or intangible properties owned by a business. The rights or claims to those assets are **equities.** Owners

2

and creditors provide resources that enable a business to purchase assets and therefore are said to have **equity** in that business. For instance, an owner may start a business with $10,000 cash. This cash is used to buy equipment. The owner, who provided the funds for the equipment, has a claim to that equipment.

The relation between assets and equities is shown by the equation:

$$\text{Assets} = \text{Equities}$$

Equities can be subdivided into two categories: (1) **Liabilities**: rights of creditors represented by debts of the business, and (2) **Owner's Equity**: rights of the owner or owners.

1.5   EXPANDING THE ACCOUNTING EQUATION

Expanding the original equation by using the two categories of equities shown in 1.4 yields the **accounting equation:**

$$\text{Assets} = \text{Liabilities} + \text{Owner's Equity}$$

Creditors have preferential rights to the assets of a corporation. The residual claim of the owner or owners may be better understood by restating the accounting equation as:

$$\text{Assets} - \text{Liabilities} = \text{Owner's Equity}$$

The dollar totals of both sides of the accounting equation are always equal, since they are simply two views of the same business property. The list of assets provides a description of the various business properties, while the list of liabilities and equity indicates the funding source for those assets.

1.6 TRANSACTIONS

A transaction can be defined as an occurrence or an event that must be recorded. Any business transaction can be stated in terms of the resulting change in the three basic elements of the accounting equation. The equality of the two sides of the accounting equation must be maintained upon completion of a transaction.

As an illustration, examine the result of a transaction to purchase land for $10,000 cash.

Assets (+$10,000 land – $10,000 cash) =
Liabilities + Owner's Equity

In this case, assets would be increased by $10,000 to reflect the land purchase and decreased by $10,000 to reflect cash paid. The net effect on assets is zero, so the accounting equation remains valid.

As another example, modify the transaction above to reflect the purchase of land by borrowing $10,000 purchase price with a bank loan (also known as a note payable).

Assets (+$10,000 land) = Liabilities (+$10,000 note payable) +
Owner's Equity

In this case, assets and liabilities are each increased by $10,000. The accounting equation therefore remains in balance.

1.7 ACCOUNTING STATEMENTS

As defined in 1.1, one of the major concerns of accounting is the preparation of summarized reports of recorded data. The principal statements used to communicate summarized data are the income statement, the statement of owner's equity, and the balance sheet. A brief description of each statement follows:

INCOME STATEMENT:

A summary of the revenue and expenses of a business entity for a specific period of time, such as a month or a year. If total revenues for the period in question exceed total expenses, the result is net income (or net profit). If total expenses exceed total revenues, the result is a net loss.

STATEMENT OF OWNER'S EQUITY:

A summary of the changes in the owner's equity of a business entity for a specific period of time, such as a month or a year. In a corporation, the emphasis is on reports of changes in retained earnings (net income retained in the business). Those changes are reported in the retained earnings statement.

BALANCE SHEET:

A list of the assets, liabilities and owner's equity of a business entity as of a specific date, usually at the close of the last day of a month or a year. Assets are usually listed first, followed by a list of liabilities and a section detailing owner's equity. Asset accounts (known as the left-hand side of the balance sheet) carry debit balances. Assets are usually listed with cash first, followed by accounts receivable, inventory, and other assets considered to be "current assets" (those easily converted to cash or expected to be converted to cash within one year). These are subtotaled and followed by a list of long-term assets such as land and equipment.

Liabilities are classified similarly. "Current liabilities" (those due within one year) are listed first, usually in the order of accounts payable, notes payable, and various other obligations such as salaries payable. These are subtotaled and followed by a listing of long-term liabilities (those due after one year). Liabilities and owner's equity (known as the right-hand side of the balance sheet) carry credit balances. Table 1.7.1 reflects the proper classification of accounts and balance sheet format.

TABLE 1.7.1

SAMPLE COMPANY
BALANCE SHEET
December 31, 1988

Current Assets:

Cash
Accounts receivable
Notes receivable
Marketable securities
Inventory
Prepaid expenses
  Total Current Assets

Long-term Assets:

Land
Office Equipment
Plant and equipment
  Total Property, Plant and
    Equipment
  Total Long-term Assets

Other Assets:

Goodwill
Intangible assets
  Total Other Assets

  Total Assets

Current Liabilities:

Accounts payable
Notes payable
  (includes current portion
    of long-term debt)
Other payables
  Total Current Liabilities

Long-term Liabilities:

Notes payable
  (net of current portion)
Bonds payable
  Total Long-term Liabilities

  Total Liabilities

Owner's Equity:

Capital stock
Retained earnings
  Total Owner's Equity

  **Total Liabilities and
  Owner's Equity**

STATEMENT OF CASH FLOWS:

The statement of cash flows is an important supplemental financial statement. This statement summarizes cash receipts and cash disbursements for a business during a given period of time, such as a month or a year. This statement supplements the income statement (which may be prepared on an accrual basis), providing users with information about an entity's ability (or inability) to meet its current cash obligations.

CHAPTER 2

THE ACCOUNTING CYCLE

2.1 ACCOUNTS

Transactions of a business are entered into **accounts.** The minimum parts of an account are:

> Title — The name of items recorded in the account
> Space for debits — Left side
> Space for credits — Right side

In its simplest form, an account can be illustrated using a T format. A **T account** is shown in Example 2.1.1.

EXAMPLE 2.1.1

Account Title

debits	credits

A complete set of accounts for a business is referred to as a **ledger.**

Debit is usually abbreviated **Dr.**

Credit is usually abbreviated **Cr.**

Debiting an account is often referred to as **charging** the account.

2.2   RECORDING TRANSACTIONS

The first step in the accounting cycle is the execution of a **transaction.** Information pertaining to the transaction is then placed on a **document.** Utilizing the debit and credit scheme, the transaction is then recorded in the **journal.** Journalizing requires that the transaction is analyzed to determine which accounts are affected, whether the effect is an increase or decrease, and finally, if this increase or decrease is represented by a debit or credit. Example 2.2.1 illustrates a simple journal format.

EXAMPLE 2.2.1

On June 1st, land costing $4,500 was purchased with cash.

Date	Account Name	Post	Debit	Credit
June 1	Land	51	4,500	
	Cash	1		4,500

The numbers in the post column are the account numbers. This number is recorded when the separate debits and credits are posted in the proper ledger accounts.

After a transaction is **journalized** (entered in the journal), the information is **posted** (recorded in the ledger). A simple ledger is illustrated in example 2.2.2.

EXAMPLE 2.2.2

ACCOUNT Cash   **Account No. 1**
                                                            Balance

Date	Item	Post	Debit	Credit	Debit	Credit
June 1		1		4,500		4,500

ACCOUNT Land   **Account No. 51**
                                                            Balance

Date	Item	Post	Debit	Credit	Debit	Credit
June 1		51	4,500		4,500	

The flow of information in the recording process can be graphically illustrated as follows:

Transaction	Document	Recorded in	Posted in
takes place	prepared	**Journal**	**Ledger**

2.3   ACCOUNT BALANCES

The balance of an account is calculated by summing both sides individually and finding the difference between the totals for each side as shown in Example 2.3.1.

EXAMPLE 2.3.1

Accounts Receivable

450	250
1,000	300
700	800
2,150	400
	1,750

Balance is a $400 debit

10

The usual balance, and effect of debits and credits on groups of accounts is shown in Table 2.3.1.

TABLE 2.3.1

	Usual Balance	Debit	Credit
Balance-sheet accounts:			
Assets	Debit	Increase	Decrease
Liabilities	Credit	Decrease	Increase
Owner's Equity	Credit	Decrease	Increase
Income-statement accounts:			
Revenue	Credit	Decrease	Increase
Expense	Debit	Increase	Decrease

CHAPTER 3

ADJUSTING ENTRIES

3.1 CASH BASIS OF ACCOUNTING

Businesses may use either the cash basis or the accrual basis of accounting to report revenues and expenses. Using the cash basis of accounting, a business would report revenues only when cash is received and expenses only when cash is disbursed. Net income is the difference between cash receipts and disbursements. This method may be acceptable for some small businesses, but its use is generally discouraged.

3.2 ACCRUAL BASIS OF ACCOUNTING

Businesses using the accrual basis of accounting report revenues in the period in which they are earned (even if the cash is received in the next accounting period). Under this basis, expenses are reported in the period in which they are incurred, not when cash is paid out.

As an example, assume that a business reports income and expenses on a monthly basis. Revenue from December sales would be reported as income during that month although cash for those sales may not be received until January (the next accounting period). Expenses are recognized monthly as they are incurred. Generally Accepted Accounting Principles require the use of the accrual basis so that revenues recognized during a given accounting period are **matched** with related expenses incurred in that same period. This process if facilitated by an adjusting process performed at the end of each accounting period.

3.3   THE ADJUSTING PROCESS

3.3.1   ADJUSTMENT OF PREPAID ASSET ACCOUNTS

Many accounts do not require adjustment at the end of an accounting period. Accounts that are usually updated upon each transaction such as cash, accounts receivable or accounts payable, will probably reflect the true existing balance at the end of a period. Some accounts, however, are not ordinarily updated except at the end of a period. Insurance premiums are usually paid in advance, creating a prepaid insurance account. These premiums are amortized (or used) in equal portions each day of the accounting period. Most businesses forego making daily entries to reflect this "usage" and simply adjust the balance at the end of the period by crediting prepaid insurance and debiting insurance expense as shown in the T accounts below. Assume that insurance premiums for six months total $600 and are paid on January 1. Each month's "usage" will be $100. At the end of January, the prepaid insurance and insurance expense accounts are adjusted to reflect the $100 charge by debiting insurance expense and crediting prepaid insurance.

EXAMPLE 3.3.1

Prepaid Insurance				Insurance Expense		
1/1	600	1/31	100	1/31	100	
1/31	500					

13

After the adjustment, the prepaid insurance account has a debit balance of $500 and insurance expense has a debit balance of $100.

3.3.2 ADJUSTMENT OF ASSET ACCOUNTS

Many businesses are unlikely to record the use of supplies each day, preferring to adjust the account at the end of the period. Supplies usage can be determined in this case by subtracting the amount of supplies on hand at the end of the period from supplies available during the period. To illustrate, assume a balance of $750 in supplies as of January 1. $500 in supplies were purchased on January 20th, so available supplies during the period are $1,250. A physical count on January 31st indicates a balance of $800. Supplies used during January must then be $450 ($1,250 – $800). The adjusting entry would be a debit to supplies expense and a credit to supplies of $450 each as shown in Example 3.3.2.

EXAMPLE 3.3.2

Supplies				Supplies Expense		
1/1	750	1/31	450	1/31	450	
1/20	500					
1/31	800					

After the adjustment, the supplies account reflects a debit balance of $800 and supplies expense reflects a balance of $450.

3.3.3 ADJUSTMENT OF PLANT ASSET ACCOUNTS

Plant assets like equipment are not "used up" like supplies, but equipment does suffer a loss in usefulness over its lifetime. This loss is a business expense known as **depreciation.** The adjusting process for depreciation expense is similar to those previously discussed, with one notable difference. It is common practice to

14

report plant assets at their original cost along with the amount of depreciation accumulated since their acquisition. As before, the amount of depreciation expense for the period is reflected as a debit to depreciation expense, but instead of crediting the asset account, a **contra-asset** account called accumulated depreciation is credited. To illustrate, equipment is purchased on January 1st for $12,000 with a useful life of 10 years. Depreciation expense is calculated at $100 per month since the equipment is assumed to have no residual value. The required adjusting entries are shown in Example 3.3.3.

EXAMPLE 3.3.3

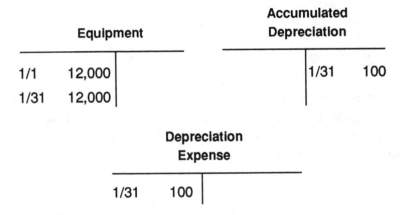

After adjustment, the balance in the equipment account is unchanged. Depreciation expense is debited for $100 and accumulated depreciation is credited for $100. The depreciable balance of equipment is now $11,900 ($12,000 cost – $100 accumulated depreciation). This is the **book value** of the equipment.

3.3.4 ADJUSTMENT OF LIABILITY ACCOUNTS

Liabilities can also require adjustment. If an accounting period, for instance, should end between payment periods, it would be proper to record the amount of wages due at the end of the accounting period. Wage expense accumulates as a liability each day and can be referred to as an accrued expense. To illustrate, assume employee wages total $20,000 each bi-weekly pay period. In this case, the accounting period ends between payment dates. The adjusting entry will be a debit to wage expense and a credit to wages payable for the amount of wages accrued as of 1/31 ($10,000), as shown in Example 3.3.4.

EXAMPLE 3.3.4

Wage Expense				Wages Payable	
1/10	20,000			1/31	10,000
1/21	20,000				
1/31	10,000				
1/31	50,000				

After the adjustment, the balance in the wage expense account is $50,000 (the true amount of expense for the month), while wages payable reflect the amount of liability for wages owned as of January 31st ($10,000).

CHAPTER 4

CLOSING ENTRIES

4.1   DEFINITION AND PURPOSE OF CLOSING ENTRIES

Closing entries are used to classify and summarize all **revenue** and **expense** accounts. Each expense and revenue account is completely cleared (leaving a zero balance) at the end of the accounting cycle. These accounts are temporary holding accounts whose balances should be transferred to an account that is permanent in nature. This would be the capital (retained earnings) account. The accumulation of new amounts of revenues and expenses begins at the start of each new accounting period.

These accounts are closed (transferred) to a summary account called **revenue and expense summary.** The revenue and expense summary account is then closed to the capital (retained earnings) account.

Ideally, closing should take place after an organization's busy period. At this time, inventories should be low and liquidity should be high. Drawing (dividends) accounts are also closed at the end of the accounting cycle.

The effect of closing entries is to bring to zero all accounts that affect the income statement. Accounts that are closed will not show any balances in the balance sheet.

4.2 STEPS IN CLOSING ENTRIES

As in other parts of the recording process of the accounting cycle, the closing of accounts involves both the **recording** of entries in the journal, and then the **posting** of the amounts and explanations in the ledger.

Revenue accounts normally have a credit balance and expense accounts normally have a debit balance. When closing accounts, an amount will be debited (revenue) or credited (expense) to the account to leave a zero balance. A like amount will be entered into the revenue and expense summary account.

The steps needed to close accounts and transfer amounts to the revenue and expense summary are summarized in Table 4.2.1.

TABLE 4.2.1

Type of Account	Entry in Account	Entry in Revenue and Expense Summary
Revenue	Debit	Credit
Expense	Credit	Debit

The entries to close the revenue and expense summary account will depend on whether the revenues were greater than expenses, or vice versa. This relationship is summarized in Table 4.2.2

TABLE 4.2.2

	Entry in Revenue and Expense Summary	Entry in Capital Account (Retained Earnings)
Revenues > Expenses	Debit	Credit
Expenses > Revenues	Credit	Debit

4.3 AN EXTENDED EXAMPLE

The following information is available before the closing process is started:

Sales Revenue		Interest Revenue		Wages Expense	
	1/12 120		1/30 40	1/15 100	
	1/19 80			1/30 30	
	1/25 30				

Rent Expense		Revenue and Expense Summary		Capital (Retained Earnings)	
1/1 20					1/1 330
1/15 130					

4.3.1 CLOSING REVENUE AND EXPENSE ACCOUNTS

The entries to close the revenue and expense accounts as of January 31st would be:

Date	Description	Debit	Credit
1/31	Sales Revenue	230	
	Revenue and Expense Summary		230
	Interest Revenue	40	
	Revenue and Expense Summary		40
	Revenue and Expense Summary	130	
	Wages Expense		130
	Revenue and Expense Summary	150	
	Rent Expense		150

These entries can be combined. If this was done the entry for both revenue accounts would be:

Date	Description	Debit	Credit
1/31	Sales Revenue	230	
	Interest Revenue	40	
	Revenue and Expense Summary		270

However, for purposes of this book, we will always make single entries. The accounts after the revenue and expense accounts are closed will be as follows:

Sales Revenue		Interest Revenue		Wages Expense	
1/31 230	1/12 120	1/31 40	1/30 40	1/15 100	1/31 130
	1/19 80			1/30 30	
	1/25 30				
230	230	40	40	130	130

Rent Expense		Revenue and Expense Summary		Capital (Retained Earnings)	
1/1 20	1/31 150	1/31 130	1/31 230		1/1 330
1/15 130		1/31 150	1/31 40		
150	150				

4.3.2 CLOSING THE REVENUE AND EXPENSE SUMMARY

The entry to close the revenue and expense summary would be:

Date	Description	Debit	Credit
1/31	Capital (Retained Earnings)	10	
	Revenue and Expense Summary		10

After this last entry is made this is the way the accounts will look:

Sales Revenue		Interest Revenue		Wages Expense	
1/31 230	1/12 120	1/31 40	1/30 40	1/15 100	1/31 130
	1/19 80			1/30 30	
	1/25 30				
230	230	40	40	130	130

Rent Expense		Revenue and Expense Summary		Capital (Retained Earnings)	
1/1 20	1/31 150	1/31 130	1/31 230	1/31 10	1/1 330
1/15 130		1/31 150	1/31 40		
150	150	280	270		Bal. 320

4.3.3 EFFECT ON CAPITAL (RETAINED EARNINGS)

As can be seen, the net effect of all the closing entries is to reduce Capital (Retained Earnings) by $10, from $330 to $320. This agrees with the following analysis:

Revenues:			Expenses:		
1/12	Sales Revenue	$120	1/1	Rent Expense	$20
1/19	Sales Revenue	80	1/15	Rent Expense	130
1/25	Sales Revenue	30	1/15	Wages Expense	100
1/30	Interest revenue	40	1/30	Wages Expense	30
	Total Revenues	$270		Total Expenses	$280

Total Revenues	$270
Total Expenses	−280
Income	$ (10)

Since there was a loss, Capital (Retained Earnings) is reduced.

CHAPTER 5

THE WORK SHEET

5.1 THE WORK SHEET

At the end of an accounting period, a number of actions are necessary. A trial balance must be constructed, adjusting entries must be journalized and posted, closing entries must be journalized and posted, and financial statements must be prepared. To simplify these procedures and to aid in eliminating errors, a **work sheet** is used. A **work sheet** is a columnar sheet of paper designed to arrange accounting data required at the end of a period in a convenient and systematic manner. This **work sheet,** as shown in Example 5.2.1, contains five pairs of columns with each pair consisting of a debit and credit column.

5.2 WORK SHEET PROCEDURES

The procedures for preparing a work sheet are as follows:

1. Ledger account balances at the end of the month are entered in the trial balance columns. The debit and credit columns are then totaled.

2. Required period-end adjustments are then entered in

EXAMPLE 5.2.1

SAMPLE COMPANY
Work Sheet
For the month ended January 31, 198x

	Trial Balance		Adjustments	
	Debit	**Credit**	**Debit**	**Credit**
Cash	12000			
Accounts Receivable	25000			
Prepaid Insurance	600			(a) 100
Office Supplies	1250			(b) 450
Equipment	12000			
Accumulated Depreciation				(c) 100
Accounts Payable		10000		
Wages Payable				(d)10000
Capital Stock		5000		
Retained Earnings		15850		
Sales Revenue		60000		
Supplies Expense			(b) 450	
Insurance Expense			(a) 100	
Depreciation Expense			(c) 100	
Wage Expense		40000	(d)10000	
Total	90850	90850	10650	10650
Net Income				
Total				

24

Adjusted Trial Balance		Income Statement		Balance Sheet	
Debit	Credit	Debit	Credit	Debit	Credit
12000				12000	
25000				25000	
500				500	
800				800	
12000				12000	
	100				100
	10000				10000
	10000				10000
	5000				5000
	15850				15850
	60000		60000		
450		450			
100		100			
100		100			
50000		50000			
100950	100950	50650	60000	50300	40950
		9350			9350
		60000	60000	50300	50300

the Adjustments columns. As a cross reference, the debit and credit parts of each adjusting entry are keyed together by placing a key letter to the left of each amount.

3.   The adjusted account balances are then entered in the Adjusted Trial Balance columns. Each account balance in the first two columns is combined with any necessary adjusting entry through horizontal addition or subtraction.

4.   Each account balance is then extended in the appropriate balance sheet or income statement column. Assets, liabilities, and owner's equity (or stockholder's equity if a corporation) accounts are balance sheet accounts. Revenue and expense accounts are income statement accounts. Each amount in the Adjusted Trial Balance columns is extended to only one of the four remaining columns.

5.   The Balance Sheet and Income Statement accounts are then totaled. The difference between debit and credit columns will determine whether the result of the company's operations for the period is a profit or loss. If credits to income accounts exceed debits to expense accounts, the result is a net profit; if debits exceed credits, the result is a net loss. This amount is entered as a debit or credit as needed to balance the debit and credit columns of the income statement and balance sheet. The columns are then totaled. All of the paired debit and credit columns should total to equal amounts.

Using the example adjusting entries from Chapter 3, four adjustments are illustrated in Example 5.2.1. These adjusting entries are reflected in the Adjustments columns of the worksheet. The effects of these adjustments are then reflected in the Adjusted Trial Balance columns. As an example, note that Prepaid Insurance began with a balance of $600. A credit of $100 was applied to this account as a result of an adjusting entry, resulting in an adjusted balance of $500. Since Prepaid Insurance is an asset

26

account, this amount is carried across to the debit column of the Balance Sheet section. The other part of this entry, reflected as a credit of $100 to Insurance Expense, is shown in the debit column of Adjustments. This amount is carried to an Adjusted Trial Balance and to the debit column of the Income Statement section. The other three adjustments reflected on this work sheet are handled similarly.

CHAPTER 6

ACCOUNTING FOR A MERCHANDISING OPERATION

6.1 GROSS PROFIT/MARGIN

Gross profit and **gross margin** are terms used interchangeably to denote the difference between the amount of sales and the **cost of goods sold**. The general format for the top part of the income statement is usually as shown in Example 6.1.1.

EXAMPLE 6.1.1

Sales	$300
Less Cost of Goods Sold	200
Gross Profit/Gross Margin	$100

6.2 PERPETUAL AND PERIODIC ACCOUNTING SYSTEMS

There are two basic ways to set up inventory systems to process the flow of information about purchases and sales. These are known as **perpetual** and **periodic** accounting systems.

6.2.1 ENTRIES UNDER PERPETUAL ACCOUNTING SYSTEMS

When utilizing **perpetual**, each purchase and sale transaction has a two-step entry. Sales entries directly affect the **cost of goods sold** account. Assuming that merchandise costing $350 was purchased, and one-half of that merchandise was sold for $300, the necessary entries are shown in Example 6.2.1.

EXAMPLE 6.2.1

Date	Description	Debit	Credit
	Merchandise Inventory Cash or Accounts Payable	350	350

To record purchase of merchandise

Date	Description	Debit	Credit
	Cash (or some other asset) Sales	300	300

To record sales of merchandise

If the merchandise is sold for cash, then cash would be debited. If instead, a promise to pay later was made, accounts or notes receivable would be debited.

Additionally, there an entry is needed to adjust both inventory and cost of goods sold as shown in Example 6.2.2.

EXAMPLE 6.2.2

Date	Description	Debit	Credit
	Cost of Goods Sold ($350 x 1/2)	175	
	Inventory		175

Under this method, inventory should always be determinable by looking in the records. Even when using this method, a physical inventory should be taken at least once each accounting cycle to assure the accuracy of the records.

6.2.2 ENTRIES UNDER PERIODIC ACCOUNTING SYSTEMS

Using the transaction from the previous section, the entries under a periodic accounting system are shown in Example 6.2.3.

EXAMPLE 6.2.3

Date	Description	Debit	Credit
	Purchases	350	
	Cash or Accounts Payable		350

To record purchase of merchandise.

	Cash (or some other asset)	300	
	Sales		300

To record sale of merchandise.

Using this method, no entries are made to adjust the inventory and cost of goods sold upon sale. These adjustments are made at the end of the accounting period. Inventory will be debited for the ending inventory amount and credited with the amount of beginning inventory. This will leave as a balance the amount of the ending physical inventory.

The calculation to determine **cost of goods sold** is shown in Example 6.2.4.

EXAMPLE 6.2.4

Merchandise Inventory – Beginning of Year	$150
Add Purchases During the Year	350
Total Goods Available for Sale	$500
Deduct Merchandise Inventory – End of Year	325
Cost of Goods Sold	$175

6.3   TRANSPORTATION CHARGES

Transportation charges are of two types. Charges for transporting merchandise to the company are **freight in**. This will be an additional cost of acquiring the goods. Outward bound charges to transport goods the firm sold are **freight out**. These are shown as **shipping expense** (a form of selling expense).

F.O.B. destination means that shipping charges are free at the destination. The charges are borne by the seller.

F.O.B. shipping point means that the seller delivers the merchandise to the carrier. However, the purchaser bears the cost of the transportation charges.

6.4   MERCHANDISE RETURNS

Nearly every business has some merchandise that is returned. This may be due to quality, color or some other factor. The seller will call these **sales returns,** while the buyer calls them **purchase returns.** The journal entry to record a return on the seller's books is shown in Example 6.4.1.

EXAMPLE 6.4.1

Date	Description	Debit	Credit
	Sales Returns and Allowances Cash (or some other asset)	10	10

Example 6.4.2 reflects the entry on the books of the buyer.

EXAMPLE 6.4.2

Date	Description	Debit	Credit
	Cash (or Accounts Payable) Purchase Returns and Allowances	10	10

6.5   MERCHANDISE ALLOWANCES

Subsequent to a sale, some merchandise can become subject to a reduced price. To the seller, this would be a **sales allowance** and to the buyer this would be a **purchase allowance**.

Entries to record merchandise allowances are identical to those for returns. Usually returns and allowances are grouped into the same account. It is important to keep them separate from sales so analysis can be done on the level of returns and allowances in relation to total sales and purchases.

6.6 TRADE DISCOUNTS

Trade discounts are price concessions made to certain buyers where the actual price charged is less than the **list price**. No entries are required since sales are recorded at actual price, not the list price.

6.7 SALES DISCOUNTS

Cash discounts are deductions allowed to customers to encourage them to pay their bills in a timely manner. These discounts are usually stated as: 2/10; n/30. This means a discount of 2% is available if paid within 10 days, but after that time, the customers must pay the full amount. Assume a sales discount was given for the $300 sale described above. If the customer paid within the ten days, the entry to record the receipt of the cash is shown in Example 6.7.1.

EXAMPLE 6.7.1

Date	Description	Debit	Credit
	Cash	294	
	Sales Discounts and Allowances	6	
	($300 x 2%)		
	Accounts Receivable		300

6.8 DETAILED INCOME STATEMENT

An income statement illustrating all of the items covered in this chapter follows in Example 6.8.1 (all numbers are assumed).

EXAMPLE 6.8.1

Gross Sales			$400
Less: Sales Returns and Allowances		$ 20	
Sales Discounts		10	30
Net Sales			$370
Cost of Goods Sold:			
Inventory January 1, 1990		$130	
Purchases	$100		
Less: Purchase Returns	$ 15		
Purchase Discounts	25	40	
Net Purchases		$ 60	
Add: Freight In		25	
Cost of Merchandise Purchased			85
Cost of Goods Available for Sale			$215
Deduct: Inventory January 31, 1990			105
Cost of Goods Sold			110
Gross Profit (or Margin)			$260

CHAPTER 7

INTERNAL CONTROL AND SPECIALIZED JOURNALS

7.1 TYPES OF INTERNAL CONTROL

Internal controls can be characterized as **internal administrative controls** or **internal accounting controls. Internal administrative controls** are those procedures and records that can assist management to reach business goals.

Internal accounting controls are those procedures and records that are concerned primarily with the **reliability** of financial records and reports, as well as safeguarding of assets.

7.2 PERSONNEL CONTROLS

An organization cannot function properly without **competent employees.** This process should begin with selection of employees who have the necessary skills and intelligence to perform the job assignment. All employees should then be provided with adequate training and supervision in order to accomplish their assigned tasks in the most efficient manner.

Employee responsibilities must be clearly defined. This encourages efficiency and helps to avoid employee confusion.

Overlapping or ill-defined job responsibilities can sometimes lead to errors or irregularities.

Employees should be **rotated** to different jobs within an organization periodically. This procedure provides several benefits. First, employees gain a larger understanding of the overall organization. In addition, it can increase both the value of an employee as well as provide management with a good deal of flexibility since employees are familiar with more than one job. This process can also strengthen the organization since irregularities or deviations from standard operating policies will be discovered when employees are rotated. In fact, employee rotation may discourage irregular practices since the employee is aware that someone else will be reviewing their work very shortly.

7.3   RECORDS CONTROL

An employee given responsibility or custodianship of an asset should not be the employee charged with maintenance of records for that asset. As an example, it is good practice to avoid a situation where an employee responsible for maintaining payroll records can also sign payroll checks.

Proper control of an organization's assets cannot be maintained without **adequate** records. This requires careful design of an accounting information system to ensure that such information is available for management on a timely basis and that the information provided is accurate.

All general ledger accounts must be **reconciled** or compared with subsidiary ledgers at the end of each accounting period. Any differences between the two balances must be investigated and explained so that errors or irregularities can be identified and corrected. In addition, account records which involve physical assets such as inventory, equipment or supplies should also be periodically reconciled with a physical count of those assets.

Periodic internal audits by organization employees may be used to discover errors or irregularities, to determine if policies and procedures are being followed, and to uncover inefficiency. As a final check and balance, an organization may use external auditors to review the existing system of internal control and make suggestions for improvement.

7.4   SPECIALIZED JOURNALS

7.4.1   PURPOSE OF SPECIALIZED JOURNALS

Many organizations often incur the same kind of transaction, such as a sale of merchandise on credit, many times during any given day. To save time, a **specialized journal** is used for that kind of transaction **only**. The most common kinds of specialized journals are the sales journal, the purchases journal, the cash receipts journal, and the cash disbursements journal. The general journal is used to record those entries that do not fit in one of these specialized journals.

7.4.2   SALES JOURNAL

The sales journal is used to record the sale of merchandise on credit **only**. This journal is illustrated in Example 7.4.2. In this example, several sales have been made on credit. Cash sales are recorded in the cash receipts journal, not the sales journal.

EXAMPLE 7.4.2

The Sample Company
Sales Journal

Date	Account Debited	Invoice No.	Ref.	Amount
1992				
Jan 2	John Jackson	222	X	1,000
6	Sally Jones	224	X	1,200
11	James Smith	225	X	900
				3,100
				(4) (80)

Each entry in the sales journal represents a debit to a customer's account. Charges to customer accounts should be posted daily and a check mark should be placed in the journal to indicate that this entry has been made.

Each entry in the sales journal also represents a credit to sales. Instead of posting a separate credit to Sales with each entry, in this example one entry is made to that account at the end of the month for the total amount of sales recorded in the sales journal.

In the illustrated example, sales on account totaled $3,100 for January. This amount is posted as a debit to accounts receivable and a credit to sales as shown in Example 7.4.3.

EXAMPLE 7.4.3

The Sample Company
General Ledger

Accounts Receivable 4		Sales 80	
1992		1992	
Jan 31 3,100		Jan 31 3,100	

Completion of this posting is noted in the sales journal by placing the account numbers of the two accounts below the total sales amount for the month.

7.4.3 PURCHASES JOURNAL

Only purchases of merchandise on credit are recorded in the purchases journal. In this instance, the term merchandise refers to goods acquired for resale to customers. Merchandise purchased for cash is recorded in the cash disbursements journal. An example of the purchases journal is shown in Example 7.4.4.

EXAMPLE 7.4.4

The Sample Company
Purchases Journal

Date	Account Credited	Invoice Date	Ref.	Credit
1992		1992		
Jan 4	Jones Company	Jan 4	X	2,400
9	Smith Corporation	8	X	5,500
13	Atlantic Supply Co.	12	X	1,300
				9,200
				(21) (9)

Each entry in the purchases journal reflects a credit to a creditor's account and a debit to purchases. Total purchases for the month ($9,200) are recorded as a debit to purchases and a credit to accounts payable as shown in Example 7.4.5.

EXAMPLE 7.4.5

The Sample Company
General Ledger

Purchases		Accounts Payable	
1992		1992	
Jan 31 9,200		Jan 31 9,200	

Completion of this journal entry is noted in the sales journal by placing the account numbers for the two accounts involved (21 for purchases and 9 for accounts payable) below the total amount of purchases for the month.

7.4.4   CASH RECEIPTS JOURNAL

All transactions involving the receipt of cash are recorded in the cash receipts journal. This journal is illustrated in Example 7.4.6. The cash receipts journal has three debit columns for cash, sales discounts, and other accounts as well as three credit columns for accounts receivable, sales and other accounts.

The use of the debit columns for cash and sales discounts are self-explanatory. The debit column for other accounts may be used when cash is received in combination with some other asset.

The credit column for accounts receivable is used to record credits to customers' accounts as receivables are collected. The credit column for sales is used to accumulate cash sales during the month so that the total can be posted to the sales account. The credit column for other accounts may be used when a transaction may require credits to two different accounts.

The following transactions are recorded in the cash receipts journal shown in Example 7.4.6:

1999

Jan 2   Sold merchandise for cash in amount of $1,000.

Jan 11   Collected $1,200 from John Jackson for sale on
           January 4.

Jan. 22 Sold land for $9,000 cash. Original cost of
           the land was $7,000.

At the end of the month, the journal columns for cash, sales discounts, accounts receivable, and sales are totaled and posted to the proper general ledger accounts. Completion of these entries is indicated by placing the corresponding general ledger account number below the column total. The totals of the other accounts columns are not posted since the individual items have already been posted. An X is placed below these columns to show that no posting is necessary.

EXAMPLE 7.4.6

Cash Receipts Journal

Date	Description	Post Ref.	Sundry Accts Credit	Sales Credit	Accts Rec. Credit	Sales Disc. Credit	Cash Debit
1999							
Jan 2	Sales			1,000			1,000
Jan 11	J. Jackson	101			1,200		1,200
Jan 22	Land	51	7,000				9,000
	Gain on						
	Land sale	85	2,000				
				1,000	1,200		11,200
				(80)	(4)		(1)

7.4.5   CASH DISBURSEMENTS JOURNAL

All payments of cash are recorded in the cash disbursements journal. Like the cash receipts journal, the cash disbursements journal contains three credit columns for cash, purchase discounts, and other accounts as well as three debit columns for accounts payable, purchases, and other accounts. The following transactions are shown in Example 7.4.7:

1992
Jan 4   Paid $800 cash for merchandise.
Jan 7   Paid Jones Company for invoice of $2,400
              dated Jan 4 (less 2% discount)
Jan 9   Bought equipment for $6,000 cash.

EXAMPLE 7.4.7

Cash Disbursements Journal

Date	Ck No.	Description	Post Ref.	Sundry Accts Debit	Accts Pay. Debit	Pur. Dis. Credit	Cash Credit
1992							
Jan 4	1	Purchases	90	800			800
Jan 7	2	Jones Co.	201		2,352	48	2,400
Jan 9	3	Equipment	52	6,000			6,000
					2,352	48	9,200
					(60)	(91)	(4)

The columns for cash, purchase discounts, accounts payable, and purchases are totaled at the end of each month and these amounts posted to the appropriate general ledger accounts. The completion of these entries is noted in the cash disbursements journal by placing the appropriate general ledger account number below the total of each column. Since items in the other accounts columns are posted individually, the totals of these columns are not posted. Accordingly, an X is placed below the total of these columns to indicate that the total was not posted.

7.4.7 SUBSIDIARY LEDGERS

The preceding sections have dealt with the use of specialized journals as information sources for entries to general ledger accounts such as cash, accounts receivable and payable, purchases, and sales. In some cases, a business may need more detailed information, such as individual customer receivable balances or the amount owed to a particular vendor. This is accomplished through the use of **subsidiary ledgers.**

For example, a business might maintain an accounts receivable ledger consisting of separate ledger accounts for each customer, arranged alphabetically or by account number. Each entry to the sales journal or to the cash receipts journal (if the transaction was a collection of a receivable) would be posted to the appropriate customer ledger so customer records would be constantly updated. At the end of the month, the total of the subsidiary ledger accounts should balance to the controlling account (the general ledger account). A similar process could be used for individual vendors (using the purchases and cash disbursements journal) or for any general ledger account that involves subsidiary accounts.

CHAPTER 8

CASH

8.1 DEFINITION OF CASH

In accounting, **cash** is paper money, coin, bank balances or other media of exchange such as bank drafts, checks or postal money orders. Postage stamps are a prepaid expense, not cash. I.O.U.'s are receivables.

In most cases, cash is a current asset. However, if there is some reason the funds are restricted, the amount of restricted cash would then be excluded from the Current Assets section of the balance sheet. This would be true of funds in an insolvent bank or compensating balances required by lending banks.

8.2 INTERNAL CONTROL AND CASH

As noted in the previous chapter, internal control should be especially well-organized with respect to cash. Because cash is so difficult to trace and easily stolen, special consideration should be given to this area of internal control.

As a result of the ease with which cash can be stolen, organizations that handle much currency like gaming establishments and bars are particularly vulnerable to **skimming**. Skimming involves the failure to report all cash receipts in order to evade income taxes. A few special controls for cash can assist the firm in controlling this very easily stolen resource. The following list will go a long way in assuring security of cash:

1. Establish a definite routine for handling of cash and separate duties so that collusion would be required to conceal a theft.

2. Anyone involved with receiving or disbursing cash should have no access to the accounting records for those transactions. Anyone involved with recording such transactions should have no access to the cash.

3. Deposit all receipts each day. No payments should be made from daily receipts.

4. All disbursements should be made with pre-numbered checks. All checks (including spoiled) should be accounted for.

5. All bank accounts should be **reconciled** monthly.

6. A **petty cash** fund should be set up to make minor disbursements. It should be reconciled monthly.

8.3   BANK ACCOUNT RECONCILIATIONS

Usually the major amount of the cash assets of a firm is in the form of deposits with banks or other financial institutions. Realize that a debit (asset) to the bank is a credit (liability) to you. Likewise, when the bank says a credit, this will be a debit on the firms' books. This reversal in accounting terms that occurs when dealing with bank accounts often causes problems.

When doing bank reconciliations, the best procedure is to work to the **true cash balance**. This will require certain adjustments to be made to the balance shown in the bank statement. There will also be some adjustments that must be made on the books of the depositor as shown below.

8.3.1 ADJUSTMENTS TO BANK BALANCE

Numerous items will require an adjustment to the balance shown in the bank statement. These include **deposits in transit, outstanding checks**, and **errors made by the bank**. In the case of each of these items, an adjustment must be made to bring the bank balance to the **true balance**. However, none of these items will require an entry in the books of the depositor. With the exception of errors, in due time, the bank will receive notice of the reconciling items in the normal course of business.

Deposits in transit are deposits that were made in the time period being accounted for, but for some reason the bank did not record. This is usually the result of a deposit made late in the day or in the mail. This amount will be added to the **balance per bank**.

Outstanding checks are checks that have been written, but have not cleared the bank as of the date of the bank statement. This is usually the largest part of a bank reconciliation. These amounts must be subtracted from the balance per bank to arrive at the true cash amount.

Outstanding checks should be watched carefully. A continuing large amount of checks outstanding may indicate a problem in control of cash. As a good practice, all checks over six months old should be canceled and reissued. This happens when a check is lost, accidentally torn up, and for other such reasons.

Errors by the bank typically involve a problem with incorrectly recorded numbers or names. A deposit or check may be encoded incorrectly by the proof operator.

For example, if the customer number is incorrectly recorded, this will cause a deposit to be put into the wrong person's account. Both accounts (the one the check did go into and the one it was supposed to go into) are now incorrect. The account that erroneously received the deposit should subtract it from the balance per bank. The account that did not receive the expected deposit will need to add that amount to the balance per bank.

Should the error be in the encoding of the amount of a check, again the balance per bank will need to be adjusted accordingly. For instance, if a check for $23.50 was encoded by the bank in the amount of $25.30, the bank will show a balance that is understated by the differences, $25.30 − $23.50, or $1.80. Again, this will require the depositor to notify the bank of the error and to note the error in the reconciliation of the bank account. No entry is required in the books of the depositor.

8.3.2   ADJUSTMENTS TO BOOK BALANCE

Any items that require an adjustment to the depositor's book balance in a reconciliation will require entries to be recorded in the depositor's accounting records. Examples include **overdrafts, automatic deposits, automatic loans,** and **monthly service charges.** A last and perhaps special instance is **returned checks,** also known as **not sufficient funds** (NSF).

Overdrafts arise when someone writes checks for more money than is in the account. Although banks dislike this action, many allow it in certain instances. Usually there will be an additional charge if an overdraft occurs. The correct action to take when this happens is to make a deposit to cover the overdraft and make an entry for any charges incurred. The proper entry to account for these charges is shown in Example 8.3.1.

EXAMPLE 8.3.1

Date	Description	Debit	Credit
	Bank Charges – Overdraft Cash	10	10

Electronic wire transfers have made **automatic payroll bank deposits** fairly common. If this is not recorded, the depositor's books will be understated by the amount of the deposit. The proper entry to adjust for this is shown in Example 8.3.2.

EXAMPLE 8.3.2

Date	Description	Debit	Credit
	Cash Payroll Income	300	300

Many banks allow for an **automatic loan** if the amount in a depositor's account goes below a specified level. The bank will have additional charges for this service. Assuming that the bank loaned a depositor $350 on automatic loan, the depositor would make the following entry shown in Example 8.3.3.

EXAMPLE 8.3.3

Date	Description	Debit	Credit
	Cash Notes Payable – Bank	350	350

The interest on the loan would normally not be paid until the loan was paid off.

Many checking accounts have monthly **service charges** for maintaining the account records. Others have a varied list of charges depending on the level of activity in the account. This may take the form of a per check, or per transaction charge. Check printing is often included as a charge to the account. Example 8.3.4 reflects the required entry.

EXAMPLE 8.3.4

Date	Description	Debit	Credit
	Bank Service Charges Cash	15	 15

The last type of adjustment to the depositor's books involves **NSF** or **returned checks**. Usually this action will require a multiple entry. This circumstance develops when a check a depositor submitted in a deposit is presented to the bank of the person who wrote the check, and the bank will not honor the check for lack of funds. This will require an entry as shown in Example 8.3.5 to the cash account of the depositor as well as an adjustment to some other asset, usually accounts receivable.

EXAMPLE 8.3.5

Date	Description	Debit	Credit
	Accounts Receivable – A. Brown Cash in Bank	100	 100

8.3.3   A SAMPLE RECONCILIATION

Example 8.3.6 is a complete reconciliation that illustrates many of the adjustments discussed in the previous sections. The exact format is not important. It is, however, important that both the bank balance and book balance are adjusted to the **true balance.**

EXAMPLE 8.3.6

SAMPLE COMPANY
BANK RECONCILIATION
January 31, 1992

Balance per bank		$3,134
Add: Deposit in transit (1/31)		1,215
Subtotal		$4,349
Deductions:		
Outstanding Checks:		
No. 235	$ 120	
No. 334	65	
No. 736	230	
No. 880	330	745
True balance per bank		$3,604
Balance per books:		$7,159
Add: Automatic deposit not recorded		1,250
Subtotal		$8,409
Deductions:		
NSF check	$4,780	
Bank service charges	25	4,805
True balance per books		$3,604

8.4 PETTY CASH

To avoid much red tape and many small insignificant checks, most organizations use a **petty cash fund** to take care of minor disbursements. This fund is usually set up on an **Imprest** basis. That means the fund is set up with a certain amount of cash and all minor payments are made from the cash. The entry to set up the fund is shown in Example 8.4.1.

EXAMPLE 8.4.1

Date	Description	Debit	Credit
	Petty Cash	200	
	Cash in Bank		200

When there is a need to replenish the petty cash fund, a debit is made to each of the individual expenses paid from the fund, and a credit is made to Cash in Bank for the total amount to replenish the fund. Example 8.4.2 illustrates such an entry.

EXAMPLE 8.4.2

Date	Description	Debit	Credit
	Postage	23	
	Advertising	59	
	Office Supplies	29	
	Delivery Expenses	37	
	Cash in Bank		148

The only time another entry would be made to petty cash, would be when the account is closed or the amount in it is adjusted to a new level.

CHAPTER 9

RECEIVABLES

9.1 ACCOUNTS RECEIVABLE

Accounts receivable arise when a business makes sales on credit. In such cases, the sales agreement calls for payment within a certain time period and may offer a discount for payment before the due date. Whether a general journal or a specialized journal such as the sales journal is used, the journal entries for a credit sale and subsequent collection would be as shown in Example 9.1.1

EXAMPLE 9.1.1

The Sample Company
General Journal

Date	Acct. No.	Description	Debit	Credit
1992 Jan 4	4	Accounts Receivable: John Doe	1,000	
	80	Sales		1,000

To record the sale of merchandise on account to John Doe.

Jan 9	1	Cash	1,000	
	4	Accounts Receivable:		
		John Doe		1,000

To record the collection of accounts receivable from John Doe.

If a discount of 2% for payment within 10 days had been offered to John Doe, the entry of January 9 would be as shown in Example 9.1.2.

EXAMPLE 9.1.2

The Sample Company
General Journal

Date	Acct. No.	Description	Debit	Credit
1992				
Jan 9	1	Cash	980	
	81	Sales Discounts	20	
	4	Accounts Receivable:		
		John Doe		1,000

To record collection of $1,000 sale made to John Doe on January 4th less 2% discount.

A business may allow the return of merchandise by the customer for credit against their account. This is accomplished through the use of the sales returns and allowances account. For example, if the customer in the previous example, John Doe, returned merchandise for $100 credit prior to payment, accounts receivable would be adjusted through the entry shown in Example 9.1.3.

EXAMPLE 9.1.3

The Sample Company
General Journal

Date	Acct. No.	Description	Debit	Credit
1992 Jan 7	82	Sales Returns and Allowances	100	
	4	Accounts Receivable: John Doe		100

9.2 UNCOLLECTIBLE ACCOUNTS RECEIVABLE

Uncollectible accounts receivable are the accounts receivable that a company cannot collect. When the conclusion is reached that a receivable is not collectible, that amount is **written off,** or removed from the company's books. Since that sale was originally recorded as revenue, this action has the effect of reducing income.

9.2.1 ALLOWANCE METHOD OF ACCOUNTING FOR UNCOLLECTIBLE ACCOUNTS

This method is also known as the reserve method because it provides in advance for uncollectible receivables. This provision for uncollectibility is made through an adjusting entry performed at the end of a fiscal period and serves two purposes. It reduces the value of receivables to the amount of cash expected to be received and allocates the expected expense associated with this reduction to the current fiscal period.

The amount of provision to be established can be calculated

several different ways. One method involves the careful examination of each customer's account to determine the probability of collection. Those deemed questionable as to collectibility are then totaled and that amount will be used as the provision amount. A simpler method involves a percentage estimate of uncollectible accounts based on outstanding receivables. Many businesses have found that the percentage of uncollectible accounts varies little from year to year and therefore feel comfortable making provisions based on this historical figure.

Once the provision amount is established, that figure will be debited to **uncollectible accounts expense** (or **bad debts expense**) and credited to **allowance for doubtful accounts**. For example, assume that The Sample Company has outstanding accounts receivable totaling $100,000 as of December 31. After examination of the individual accounts, management believes all but $5,000 is likely to be collected. The adjusting entry to reflect the provision for uncollectible accounts is shown in Example 9.2.1.

EXAMPLE 9.2.1

The Sample Company
General Journal

Date	Acct. No.	Description	Debit	Credit
1992 Dec31	95	Uncollectible Accounts Expense	5,000	
	5	Allowance for Doubtful Accounts		5,000

The debit balance of $100,000 in outstanding accounts receivable represents total claims against customers. The net realizable value of those receivables (the amount expected to be collected) is $95,000. The amount of accounts receivable reported on the financial statement is generally the net realizable value, accompanied by a notation as to the amount of allowance for uncollectible accounts.

9.2.2 WRITE-OFFS TO THE ALLOWANCE ACCOUNT

When an account is determined to be uncollectible, that amount is charged against the allowance for uncollectible accounts. As an example, the account of Mary Smith, which has a balance of $200, is deemed to be uncollectible on May 13th. The entry to reflect this action is shown in Example 9.2.2.

EXAMPLE 9.2.2

The Sample Company
General Journal

Date	Acct. No.	Description	Debit	Credit
1992 May13	5	Allowance for Doubtful Accounts	200	
	4	Accounts Receivable: Mary Smith		200

To record write off of uncollectible account.

An account which has been written off may later be collected. In such an instance, the account should be reinstated through an entry just the reverse of that used to write off the account. To illustrate, should the account written off in Example 9.2.2 be subsequently collected, an entry to reinstate that account is shown in Example 9.2.3.

EXAMPLE 9.2.3

The Sample Company
General Journal

Date	Acct. No.	Description	Debit	Credit
1992 Jul 20	4	Accounts Receivable: Mary Smith	200	
	5	Allowance for Doubtful Accounts		200

9.3 DIRECT WRITE-OFF METHOD OF ACCOUNT-ING FOR UNCOLLECTIBLE ACCOUNTS

The allowance method of accounting for uncollectible accounts is preferred, since it allows the matching of uncollectible accounts expense with the associated revenues. There may be situations, however, where the direct write-off method may be used. There may be situations where it is not feasible to estimate the amount of uncollectible accounts or the amount may not be material. In such cases, a business may choose to adopt the direct write-off method. Under this method, an allowance account or an adjusting entry at the end of the fiscal period are not needed. When an account is deemed to be uncollectible, an entry to reflect that decision is made as shown in Example 9.3.1.

EXAMPLE 9.3.1

The Sample Company
General Journal

Date	Acct. No.	Description	Debit	Credit
1992 June 6	95 4	Uncollectible Accounts Expense Accounts Receivable: Mary Smith	25	25

To write off uncollectible account.

Subsequent recovery of an account that has been written-off would require an entry to reinstate that account. The entry would be performed in reverse manner from the entry shown in Example 9.3.1.

9.4 NOTES RECEIVABLE

Notes receivable arise when customers or others obligate themselves to a business through a formal contract to repay the face amount of a loan at a specific date with interest calculated at a specific rate. For example, assume that Paul Johnson borrows $5,000 from The Sample Company on April 4. The terms of the note require repayment within 60 days. Interest is to be calculated at 12%. The entry to reflect this transaction and subsequent payment of the loan is shown in Example 9.4.1.

EXAMPLE 9.4.1

The Sample Company
General Journal

Date	Acct. No.	Description	Debit	Credit

1992 April 4	7	Notes Receivable: Paul Johnson	5,000	
	1	Cash		5,000

To reflect loan to Paul Johnson of $5,000 for 60 days at 12%.

May 4	1	Cash	5,100	
	7	Notes Receivable: Paul Johnson		5,000
	86	Interest Income		100

To record payment of note receivable.

9.5   DISCOUNTING NOTES RECEIVABLE

A business may not wish to wait until a note receivable matures before receiving cash. In such a case, it may **discount**, or sell a note receivable to a bank. The bank obviously will not pay the full maturity value of the note and will calculate a discount based on an agreed percentage. Using the note receivable shown in Example 9.4.1, assume that The Sample Company needs the cash immediately and discounts the note to its bank on April 6. The bank charges a discount rate of 14%. The discount value of the note is calculated in Example 9.5.1.

EXAMPLE 9.5.1

Face value of the note	$5,000
Interest on note – 30 days @ 12%	100
Maturity value	5,100
Discount period April 6 to June 3: 58 days	
Discount on maturity value: 58 days @ 14%	115
Proceeds	$4,985

The journal entry to record this transaction is shown in Example 9.5.2.

EXAMPLE 9.5.2

The Sample Company
General Journal

Date	Acct. No.	Description	Debit	Credit
1992 April 6	1	Cash	4,985	
	96	Interest Expense	15	
	7	Notes Receivable		5,000

In this case, the proceeds received from discounting were less than the face value of the note. Had the proceeds exceeded the face value of the note receivable, the difference would have been interest income, instead of interest expense.

9.6   DISHONORED NOTES RECEIVABLE

When a customer fails to pay a note receivable on the due date, the note is **dishonored** and is no longer considered a valid asset of the company. In such cases, the face amount of the note receivable may be charged against an allowance account similar to that used for uncollectible accounts receivable. Any interest income that has been accrued and recorded as interest receivable would then be written off. As an alternative, the face amount of the note plus accrued interest may be converted to an account receivable and handled according to established procedures for that type of account.

CHAPTER 10

INVENTORY

10.1 INTRODUCTION TO INVENTORY ACCOUNTING

In the United States, four inventory methods have gained wide acceptance and are considered generally accepted. These methods are **FIFO, LIFO, weighted average,** and **specific identification.**

The Internal Revenue Service (IRS) requires that any businesses which re-sell merchandise inventory must keep accounting records on the accrual basis. The **consistency** convention requires that businesses not change inventory methods often.

Use of an inventory method does not mean that the physical flow of goods follows the cost flow. The methods are used to better approximate current economic conditions of the costs involved. Hence, even if an organization is using **LIFO** for inventory costing, the actual flow of physical goods could be on a **FIFO** basis.

10.2 PERIODIC AND PERPETUAL ACCOUNTING
SYSTEMS

There are two main accounting systems, **periodic** and **perpet-**

ual, for keeping track of inventory. Refer to Chapter 6 for further elaboration on this topic.

10.3   INVENTORY METHODS

Table 10.3.1 provides information to be used to demonstrate the various inventory methods:

TABLE 10.3.1

SAMPLE COMPANY
INVENTORY RECORDS

Date	Action	Units	Cost per Unit	Total Amount	Balance (In Units)
1-1	Balance	15	$10	$150	15
1-7	Purchased	30	11	330	45
1-10	Purchased	20	12	240	65
1-15	Sold	10	–	–	55
1-25	Sold	10	–	–	45
1-30	Sold	15	–	–	30
Total				$720	

When calculating inventory and cost of goods sold, there are two truths that will always hold. The total goods available for sale is equal to the sum of the ending inventory and the cost of goods sold. Using the data above, that means that ending inventory, plus the cost of goods sold will be equal to $720. Likewise the sum of the units in ending inventory and the units in cost of goods sold will total 65. By checking these numbers each time ending inventory and cost of goods sold is calculated, minor arithmetic errors can be quickly identified.

10.3.1 FIFO

The **First-in, first-out** inventory method assumes that costs are charged against revenue in the order in which they were incurred. Thus the most recent costs are assumed to still be in inventory.

Using the data given above, the results of using FIFO are shown in Example 10.3.1:

EXAMPLE 10.3.1

CALCULATIONS USING FIFO

Ending Inventory			Cost of-Goods-Sold			
Date Pur.	Cost	Total	Date Pur.	Date Sold	Cost	Total
1-10:	20x$12@ =	$240	1-1:	1-15	10x$10@ =	$100
1-7:	10x$11@ =	110	1-1:	1-25	5x$10@ =	50
			1-7:	1-25	5x$11@ =	55
			1-7:	1-30	15x$11@ =	165
Total	30	$350	Total		35	$370

As can be seen from the example, total units is equal to 65 (30 in ending inventory and 35 in cost of goods sold). Also the sum of the ending inventory and cost of goods sold is equal to $720; $350 + $370 = $720.

10.3.2 LIFO

The **Last-in, first-out** inventory method assumes that costs are charged against revenue in the **reverse** order in which they were incurred. Thus the oldest costs are assumed to still be in inventory.

Using the data given above, the results of using LIFO are shown in Example 10.3.2:

EXAMPLE 10.3.2

CALCULATIONS USING FIFO

Ending Inventory			Cost of-Goods-Sold			
Date Pur.	Cost	Total	Date Pur.	Date Sold	Cost	Total
1-1:	15x$10@ =	$150	1-15:	1-20	10x$12@ =	$120
1-7:	15x$11@ =	165	1-15:	1-25	10x$12@ =	120
			1-7:	1-30	15x$11@ =	165
Total	30	$315	Total		35	$405

As can be seen from the example, total units is equal to 65 (30 in ending inventory and 35 in cost of goods sold). Also the sum of the ending inventory and cost of goods sold is equal to $720; $315 + $405 = $720.

LIFO is allowed for income tax reporting purposes. However, the IRS requires that if LIFO is used for income tax purposes, it must also be used for financial reporting purposes.

10.3.3 WEIGHTED AVERAGE

The **weighted average method** is also sometimes called the **average cost method**. This method assumes that the same cost per unit is charged to units remaining in inventory as was charged to units that have been sold during the period. The calculations for this method are much simpler than those for FIFO and LIFO.

Using the same data, we find that the total cost of $720 divided by the total units of 65 gives a unit cost of $11.0769. Then the calculations for ending inventory and cost of goods sold are:

Ending inventory	=	30 units x $11.0769	=	$332.31
Cost of goods sold	=	35 units x $11.0769	=	387.69
Total		65		$720.00

As can be seen from the example, total units is equal to 65 (30 in ending inventory and 35 in cost of goods sold). Also the sum of the ending inventory and cost of goods sold is equal to $720; $332.31 + $387.69 = $720.

10.3.4 SPECIFIC IDENTIFICATION

When using **specific identification,** it is assumed that there is a linkage of costs with the physical units of inventory. In this case, the calculations would rely upon a direct tracing of which units were sold and which are still in inventory. Then their respective costs would be assigned. This is the only method discussed in this chapter that does trace the actual physical flow of goods.

10.3.5 REPLACEMENT COST

All of the methods discussed so far deal with **historical costs**. Within the accounting establishment, there is strong support for using the concept of **replacement cost**. This is sometimes referred to as **next-in, first-out**, or **NIFO**.

Currently, replacement cost is not allowed within **generally accepted accounting principles** or **GAAP**.

10.4 COMPARISON OF COST METHODS

Remembering that the sum of ending inventory and cost of

goods sold is equal to the total cost of goods available for sale, it is clear that a difference in ending inventory will have a like effect on cost of goods sold. Different methods will likewise produce different net income amounts.

In times of inflation (rising costs), using LIFO will reduce net income as the highest costs are charged to revenue first. FIFO on the other hand, will have the highest net income. This is because under FIFO the lowest costs are charged to revenue first.

In times of deflation (declining costs) the reverse would be true. The high inflation rates during the 1960's and 1970's increased the usage of LIFO greatly.

At the same time, weighted average net income will always be between LIFO and FIFO unless the economy has shifted from inflation to deflation or vice versa.

10.5 LOWER OF COST OR MARKET

The **conservatism convention** basically says that account-ants should use the worst estimate in terms of net income. Hence, an alternative method of valuing inventories is **lower-of-cost-or-market**. This would mandate that if the value of inventory is more than what it would cost to buy new like inventory, the inventory should be written down to market value. The loss in value would be charged to income.

If at a later date, the value of the inventory (market price) increases, the inventory would be written up to whichever is lower, current value or what it originally cost. It can never be written up above original cost.

The lower-of-cost-or-market can be applied in one of three ways. It could be applied to each item in the inventory, to major categories or classes of goods, or to the inventory as a whole.

CHAPTER 11

PROPERTY, PLANT AND EQUIPMENT

11.1 PROPERTY, PLANT AND EQUIPMENT

Property, plant and equipment describes assets such as land, building, machinery, tools, or furniture which are used in the course of business. These assets are tangible in nature and are not held for resale. Often these assets are referred to as **plant assets** or **fixed assets**. Assets acquired for resale in the normal course of business cannot be characterized as property, plant and equipment regardless of type or length of time held. Land held for speculation should be considered an investment.

11.2 COST BASIS FOR PROPERTY, PLANT AND EQUIPMENT

All costs necessary to purchase equipment and make it ready for use are included in its cost basis. Costs such as sales tax, transportation charges, insurance on the asset while in transit, and installation costs should be added to the cost basis of the associated asset. If the asset is purchased secondhand, expenses for repair or new parts should be added to the purchase price.

67

Costs such as architect's fees, surveys, insurance during construction, and interest on loans to finance construction of a building should be included in the cost basis for a building. Appropriate costs that may be added to the cost basis for land include broker's commissions, survey fees, title fees, as well as the cost of removing unwanted buildings.

11.3 DEPRECIATION

Property, plant and equipment, with the exception of land, suffers a decline in usefulness over time due to physical wear and tear or technical obsolescence. This decrease in usefulness is known as **depreciation**. Each asset has an estimated useful life, which is used to calculate the amount of depreciation expense for each period. If the asset is deemed to have no value at the end of its useful life, depreciation expense will be calculated to reduce the **book value** (cost less accumulated depreciation) to zero at the end of the asset's useful life. If the asset is expected to have some minimal or residual value at the end of its useful life, depreciation expense should be calculated to reduce the book value of an asset to its residual value at the end of its useful life. Depreciation can be calculated several different ways, such as straight-line, sum-of-the-years-digits, declining balance, and units-of-production.

11.3.1 STRAIGHT-LINE METHOD OF DEPRECIATION

The **straight-line** method of calculating depreciation is very popular due to its simplicity and because it can provide a reasonable allocation of costs to periodic revenue when usage is relatively the same from period to period. To illustrate, assume that the initial cost of an asset is $70,000, its estimated useful life is 10 years, and its residual value is $10,000. Annual depreciation would be calculated as shown in Example 11.3.1

EXAMPLE 11.3.1

Depreciable cost:

   $70,000 initial cost − $10,000 residual value = $60,000

Monthly depreciation:

$$\frac{\text{Depreciable Cost}}{\text{Estimated life}} = \frac{\$60,000}{10 \text{ years}} = \$6,000 \text{ per year}$$

11.3.2 SUM-OF-THE-YEARS-DIGITS METHOD OF DEPRE-CIATION

The **sum-of-the-years-digits** method of depreciation is an **accelerated** method of calculating depreciation in that it provides a declining depreciation charge over the life of an asset. The annual rate of depreciation is calculated by dividing the number of years left in the asset's useful life by the sum of the digits representing the years of estimated life. Using the information from Example 11.3.1, depreciation using the sum-of-the-years-digits method is shown in Example 11.3.2.

EXAMPLE 11.3.2

Depreciable cost = $60,000

Sum of the years of estimated life =
1+2+3+4+5+6+7+8+9+10 = 55

Year	Rate	Annual Depreciation	Accumulated Depreciation	Book Value
1	10/55	10,909	10,909	59,091
2	9/55	9,818	20,727	49,273

Year	Rate	Annual Depreciation	Accumulated Depreciation	Book Value
3	8/55	8,727	29,454	40,546
4	7/55	7,636	37,090	32,910
5	6/55	6,545	43,635	26,365
6	5/55	5,455	49,090	20,910
7	4/55	4,364	53,454	16,546
8	3/55	3,273	56,727	13,274
9	2/55	2,182	58,909	11,091
10	1/55	1,091	60,000	10,000

11.3.3 DECLINING BALANCE METHOD OF DEPRECIATION

Like sum-of-the-years-digits, the **declining balance** method of depreciation is an accelerated method of depreciation, providing a declining periodic depreciation charge over the estimated life of an asset. A common technique is to use the straight-line depreciation rate (from 11.1.1), doubling it (**double-declining balance method**) for application to the cost of the asset less accumulated depreciation (book value). The residual value is **not** considered in calculating annual depreciation (although the asset should not be depreciated below its estimated residual value). Using the information from previous examples, the double-declining balance method of depreciation is illustrated in Example 11.3.3.

EXAMPLE 11.3.3

Depreciation rate:

Straight-line rate is 10% per year (10 years estimated life)

10% x 2 = 20% per year for double-declining balance rate.

Cost = $70,000   Residual value = $10,000

Year	Rate	Annual Depreciation	Accumulated Depreciation	Book Value
1	20%	14,000	14,000	56,000
2	20%	11,200	25,200	44,800
3	20%	8,960	34,160	35,840
4	20%	7,168	41,328	28,672
5	20%	5,734	47,062	22,938
6	20%	4,588	51,650	18,350
7	20%	3,670	55,320	14,680
8	20%	2,936	58,256	11,744
9	20%	1,744	60,000	10,000

Since the asset cannot be depreciated below its residual value, depreciation in year 9 is limited to $1,744 instead of the calculated value of $2,349. This depreciates the asset to its residual value of $10,000. No further calculations are needed.

11.3.4 UNITS-OF-PRODUCTION METHOD

In some cases, a more equitable allocation of cost would involve dividing an asset's cost by estimated units of output rather than estimated life. For example, a business might calculate depreciation for a truck based on mileage instead of estimated life. This calculation divides the depreciable cost of the truck (initial cost – residual value) by the estimated useful life of the truck to obtain a depreciation rate per mile. To illustrate, a truck with an initial cost of $20,000 and a residual value of $5,000 has an estimated useful life of 100,000 miles. The truck has been driven 25,000 miles during this accounting period. The calculation of the depreciation rate and the annual depreciation figure are shown in Example 11.3.4.

EXAMPLE 11.3.4

$$\frac{\$20{,}000 \text{ cost} - \$5{,}000 \text{ residual value}}{100{,}000 \text{ miles} \text{ (estimated useful life)}} = \$0.15 \text{ depreciation per mile}$$

25,000 miles (current period usage) x $0.15 = $3,750

Depreciation for this accounting period is $3,750.

CHAPTER 12

OTHER LONG-TERM ASSETS

12.1 INTRODUCTION OF OTHER LONG-TERM ASSETS

In addition to plant property and equipment, there are numerous other **long-term assets** (in use more than one year), that will usually be found at the bottom of the asset side of the balance sheet. In this chapter we will review the most important of these assets. These will include **leaseholds, leasehold improvements, patents, copyrights,** and **goodwill.**

Although long-term assets that are not plant property and equipment (PPE) are not depreciated, many of them do lose value like PPE. We will also review the use of **depletion** of natural resources, as well as the **amortization** of **intangible assets.**

12.2 LEASING

There are two basic types of leases in the world of accounting. They are **operating leases** and **capital leases.** FASB Statement No. 13 very specifically spells out what conditions need to be met in order to be one kind or the other.

12.2.1 CAPITAL LEASES

Leases that have one or more of the following provisions are defined as **capital leases**:

1. The lease transfers ownership of the leased asset to the lessee at the end of the lease term.

2. The lease contains an option for a bargain purchase of the leased asset by the lessee.

3. The lease term extends over most of the economic life of the leased asset.

4. The lease requires rental payments which approximate the fair market value of the leased asset.

The capital lease is accounted for as a purchase of the asset. Consequently, when the lease is executed, the lessee will debit a fixed asset account for the fair market value of the asset, and would set up a long-term lease liability.

12.2.2 OPERATING LEASES

Operating leases are all other leases that do not meet one or more of the above conditions to be a capital lease. Operating leases are accounted for by recognizing rent expense as the leased asset is used.

12.2.3 LEASEHOLDS, AND LEASEHOLD IMPROVE- MENTS

A **leasehold** is the right to use, for a certain amount of time (more than one year), a fixed asset. This is usually a building or part of a building. A **leasehold improvement** would be any improvement made to the leasehold that may not be removed when the lease expires. Examples include new walls, central air conditioning or new fixtures.

Leaseholds and leasehold improvements are accounted for in the same manner as depreciation. However, straight-line is used as accelerated methods are not allowed for income tax purposes. This systematic write-off is called **amortization**.

When the life of the fixed asset is longer than the life of the lease, the amortization will be for the life of the lease.

12.3 DEPLETION

Accounting for the use of natural resources such as timber, oil, and metal ores is known as **depletion**. The costs for these natural resources is accounted for as fixed assets. Then the period cost (depletion) is based on the relationship of the total amount of the natural resource to the amount removed during the period.

For example, assume that a forest has been purchased to be used to provide timber for a lumber mill. The cost of purchasing this asset was $150,000. There are a total 1,500 acres of timber. During the current accounting period, 100 acres of timber were cut. The journal entry for this period is given in Example 12.3.

EXAMPLE 12.3

The Sample Company
General Journal

Date	Acct. No.	Description	Debit	Credit
1992 Apr 30	24 10	Depletion Expense – Timber Accumulated Depletion – Timber	10,000	10,000

To record the first quarter depletion of timber.

The calculation to arrive at the $10,000 figure is:

100 acres/1,500 acres = 1/15; 1/15 x $150,000 = $10,000

12.4 INTANGIBLE ASSETS

In the operations of a company there are often long-term assets that are not held for sale and do not have physical qualities. These are called **intangible assets.**

There are two major concerns in accounting for intangibles. The first problem is to determine the initial costs of the asset. Then there is the need to recognize the period of expiration of these costs. This is usually done by a process called **amortization.** Following are several types of intangible assets.

12.4.1 PATENTS

Patents are rights granted exclusively to a person or company to produce and sell a particular invention. These rights are granted for 17 years by the federal government. The costs of the patent should be debited to an asset account and then written off in a systematic manner. Unless another method can be shown to be more appropriate, straight-line amortization should be used.

If the expected useful economic life of the patent is less than 17 years, then the shorter length of time will be used for the amortization process. A contract account (such as accumulated amortization), is usually not utilized with intangibles. Amortization is written off directly to the asset.

Consider a patent that cost $300,000 to develop. It is expected that the economic life of the patent will be ten years. The entry for the first full year of amortization would be as shown in Example 12.4.1.

EXAMPLE 12.4.1

The Sample Company
General Journal

Date	Acct. No.	Description	Debit	Credit
1992 Dec31	23	Amortization Expense – Patents	30,000	
	11	Patents		30,000

To record the yearly amortization of the patent.

Each succeeding year would have a similar entry recorded. Most intangible assets have a zero residual value.

12.4.2 COPYRIGHTS

Copyrights are the exclusive rights granted to publish and sell books, artistic compositions, and musical compositions. These rights are granted by the federal government and extend to 50 years past the author's death. Copyrights are recorded at the price paid for them. They are usually amortized over very short periods – usually two to three years. The accounting for copyrights would be identical to that for patents.

12.4.3 FRANCHISES

Franchises are rights and privileges granted to sell a service or product in specified manner. These rights are usually granted by a distributor or manufacturer. Examples would be major sports teams, or MacDonald's restaurants. The accounting for franchises will be handled the same as those for patents and copyrights.

12.4.4 GOODWILL

When a company or part of a company is purchased, it is not uncommon for the purchaser to pay more than the sum of the fair market value for the individual assets minus the liabilities. This excess is called **goodwill**. It is often attributed to good management, good location, outstanding reputation, or other such factors.

This cost is treated as an intangible asset and amortized over the expected economic life of the goodwill. However, this life cannot exceed 40 years and it cannot be written off all in one lump sum.

REA's <u>Authoritative</u> Guide to

LAW SCHOOLS

Official, complete, detailed, and up-to-date profiles of accredited and non-accredited law schools in the U.S.A. and Canada

R&EA *Research & Education Association*

Available at your local bookstore or order directly from us by sending in coupon below.

MAXnotes®

REA's Literature Study Guides

MAXnotes® are student-friendly. They offer a fresh look at masterpieces of literature, presented in a lively and interesting fashion. **MAXnotes®** offer the essentials of what you should know about the work, including outlines, explanations and discussions of the plot, character lists, analyses, and historical context. **MAXnotes®** are designed to help you think independently about literary works by raising various issues and thought-provoking ideas and questions. Written by literary experts who currently teach the subject, **MAXnotes®** enhance your understanding and enjoyment of the work.

Available **MAXnotes®** include the following:

Absalom, Absalom!
The Aeneid of Virgil
Animal Farm
Antony and Cleopatra
As I Lay Dying
As You Like It
The Autobiography of
   Malcolm X
The Awakening
Beloved
Beowulf
Billy Budd
The Bluest Eye, A Novel
Brave New World
The Canterbury Tales
The Catcher in the Rye
The Color Purple
The Crucible
Death in Venice
Death of a Salesman
The Divine Comedy I: Inferno
Dubliners
Emma
Euripides' Medea & Electra
Frankenstein
Gone with the Wind
The Grapes of Wrath
Great Expectations
The Great Gatsby
Gulliver's Travels
Hamlet
Hard Times

Heart of Darkness
Henry IV, Part I
Henry V
The House on Mango Street
Huckleberry Finn
I Know Why the Caged
   Bird Sings
The Iliad
Invisible Man
Jane Eyre
Jazz
The Joy Luck Club
Jude the Obscure
Julius Caesar
King Lear
Les Misérables
Lord of the Flies
Macbeth
The Merchant of Venice
Metamorphoses of Ovid
Metamorphosis
Middlemarch
A Midsummer Night's Dream
Moby-Dick
Moll Flanders
Mrs. Dalloway
Much Ado About Nothing
My Antonia
Native Son
1984
The Odyssey
Oedipus Trilogy

Of Mice and Men
On the Road
Othello
Paradise Lost
A Passage to India
Plato's Republic
Portrait of a Lady
A Portrait of the Artist
   as a Young Man
Pride and Prejudice
A Raisin in the Sun
Richard II
Romeo and Juliet
The Scarlet Letter
Sir Gawain and the
   Green Knight
Slaughterhouse-Five
Song of Solomon
The Sound and the Fury
The Stranger
The Sun Also Rises
A Tale of Two Cities
The Taming of the Shrew
The Tempest
Tess of the D'Urbervilles
Their Eyes Were Watching God
To Kill a Mockingbird
To the Lighthouse
Twelfth Night
Uncle Tom's Cabin
Waiting for Godot
Wuthering Heights

RESEARCH & EDUCATION ASSOCIATION
61 Ethel Road W. • Piscataway, New Jersey 08854
Phone: (732) 819-8880

Please send me more information about MAXnotes®.

Name _____

Address _____

City _____ State _____ Zip _____

REA's **Problem Solvers**

The "PROBLEM SOLVERS" are comprehensive supplemental text-books designed to save time in finding solutions to problems. Each "PROBLEM SOLVER" is the first of its kind ever produced in its field. It is the product of a massive effort to illustrate almost any imaginable problem in exceptional depth, detail, and clarity. Each problem is worked out in detail with a step-by-step solution, and the problems are arranged in order of complexity from elementary to advanced. Each book is fully indexed for locating problems rapidly.

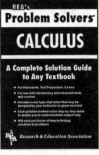

ACCOUNTING
ADVANCED CALCULUS
ALGEBRA & TRIGONOMETRY
AUTOMATIC CONTROL
  SYSTEMS/ROBOTICS
BIOLOGY
BUSINESS, ACCOUNTING, & FINANCE
CALCULUS
CHEMISTRY
COMPLEX VARIABLES
COMPUTER SCIENCE
DIFFERENTIAL EQUATIONS
ECONOMICS
ELECTRICAL MACHINES
ELECTRIC CIRCUITS
ELECTROMAGNETICS
ELECTRONIC COMMUNICATIONS
ELECTRONICS
FINITE & DISCRETE MATH
FLUID MECHANICS/DYNAMICS
GENETICS
GEOMETRY

HEAT TRANSFER
LINEAR ALGEBRA
MACHINE DESIGN
MATHEMATICS for ENGINEERS
MECHANICS
NUMERICAL ANALYSIS
OPERATIONS RESEARCH
OPTICS
ORGANIC CHEMISTRY
PHYSICAL CHEMISTRY
PHYSICS
PRE-CALCULUS
PROBABILITY
PSYCHOLOGY
STATISTICS
STRENGTH OF MATERIALS &
  MECHANICS OF SOLIDS
TECHNICAL DESIGN GRAPHICS
THERMODYNAMICS
TOPOLOGY
TRANSPORT PHENOMENA
VECTOR ANALYSIS

*If you would like more information about any of these books,
complete the coupon below and return it to us or visit your local bookstore.*

RESEARCH & EDUCATION ASSOCIATION
61 Ethel Road W. • Piscataway, New Jersey 08854
Phone: (732) 819-8880

Please send me more information about your Problem Solver books

Name _____

Address _____

City _____ State _____ Zip _____